Hope Speaking presents.

Nose to Nose Networking

No-nonsense, in-person networking with intention.

Leslie,
To the lady who
spices up my life
(and my omelettes!)

by Mélanie Hope

Happy Networking!
♡ M'Dawe

The author has taken reasonable precautions in the preparation of this book and believes that the facts presented in the book are accurate as of the date it was written. While many of these methods are indeed tried and true, results will vary by the individual's dedication and practice. Really, though, what have you got to lose? If a dog can do it, you certainly can! Still, neither the publisher nor the dog assume any responsibility for any errors or omissions and specifically disclaim any liability resulting from the use or application of the information contained in this book.

ISBN 1453721304
EAN-13 9781453721308

10 9 8 7 6 5 4 3 2 1

Designed by StormKatt Productions
www.StormKatt.com

Photography by Jim Moniz and Mélanie Hope

Contents

An introduction

A well-built network permeates nearly every aspect of both your personal and business lives. Your network is absolutely imperative for survival in the business world, makes it easier to accomplish day-to-day tasks and gives you resources for every emergency situation. With your network you can get advice on anything, fix anything, find anything, get a deal on anything and sell anything. If you don't know someone directly, your network will help you find someone who does.

Social media is all the rage, but an online network can only go so far. Meaningful networking requires leaving the safety of your home and meeting real, live people. Face-to-face networking, what was once the only way to network, has now become a source of fear and stress. Funny that in a world where we are so connected to one another we still find it difficult to actually connect.

It doesn't have to be.

Networking should be as easy and natural as petting a friendly dog. A well-trained, friendly dog is remembered and welcomed nearly everywhere. Even people who don't particularly like dogs will warm up to a good dog. Dogs, as many studies have shown, can lower your blood pressure and increase many feel-good hormones. Dogs see the real person within and are not afraid to introduce themselves to strangers. Wouldn't it be great to have those kinds of social skills? Wouldn't you love to see networking as a joy, rather than a task?

You have a warm, inviting smile. You have bright eyes and, I'm sure, a glossy coat. You know how to sit, shake and speak. We'll assume that you are well-adjusted and inherently friendly (even if a little shy) – now we'll work on getting you well-trained. What does a dog have that you don't?

As you go through this book, you will see that what seems to come naturally to a particular Golden Retriever can be easily translated into human actions and attitudes that will make you, too, a master networker.

Meet Abby

When it comes to memorable connections and the most effective networking, no one knows how to work a room better than my Golden Retriever, Abigail.

I picked Abby out of a litter of 8-week old puppies, all fat little butterballs of golden fur. I asked about the runt, the only red dog of the bunch and decided to take her home after the breeder told me that she was the only one with a 'little bit of attitude.' A redhead with an attitude? That's MY dog!

She came home with me during a tumultuous period in my life, but her sweet determination and unfailing devotion helped me (and everyone she has ever met) face even the toughest times. I recommend puppy therapy to anyone going through a divorce, illness or death of a loved one – especially if going through all three at once.

I began training Abby in both vocal and sign commands so that we could communicate comfortably both off- and on-leash. She took the lead in her social skills, attracting adults and children from all walks of life. She makes it look so easy.

She even befriended the ducks at her favorite park - they follow her (and no other dog!) around the pond.

Abby has taught me a lot about no-nonsense, old-fashioned, in-person networking with intention. If ever you take a trip to the Seattle area, head south and find a little suburb known as Kent. Go downtown and check out the shops in the historic district. Play in the fountain at Kent Station or have a chai latté at the Kona Kai. Chances are you will run into someone who knows Abby.

Abby poses for tourists at Kent Station.

Part 1
Nose-to-Nose
The definition of networking

Focus on The Ball

Turning onto Military Road, Abby's panting quickens. She knows where we are going. As we pull into Grandview Off Leash Park, she is near euphoria. This is one of her favorite places! Mom is the best! As I open the back door, she does not jump out. Instead, she turns and twists frantically as if looking for something of utmost importance. There it is! A ratty old tennis ball. Now, with ball in mouth, the adventure may begin.

No matter how excited she is, Abby NEVER forgets to grab a ball on her way to the park. She has a very clear objective: The Ball. Get folks to toss The Ball. Follow The Ball. Get The Ball. Bring back The Ball.

I also have a very clear objective: Wear out the dog. Every owner at the dog park has a similar objective.

Yes, some people have secondary objectives like losing weight and human socialization. Still, their first goal is kept quite clear – exercise the dog. Imagine going to a dog park where all dogs were kept on short leashes so they could not run and play. It would completely defeat the purpose of going.

Networking is purpose-driven. If you go into an event or any situation with no idea what you are doing or why, you will accomplish nothing. Why meet 200 real-estate agents but find no one who can help you repair your clunking car or alert you to positions in the software industry? It would completely defeat the purpose of going.

Whether going to a convention or a convenience store, always network with intention. Your objective is not to collect business cards, but to meet quality contacts that will further your business or your career and/or fill a need. In other words, focus on The Ball.

Think about your reasons for networking. Before you begin, really think about your intention. What do you ultimately hope to achieve? Write it down.

Set goals in steps. Make them measureable and achievable. You cannot work towards a goal unless and until you set one and understand what it means.

Now, decide the type of people you would like to get to know better.

Where do you need help? Are you willing to ask people for help and/ or accept it when offered? Needing help in itself is NOT a weakness. Everyone has different skills and it is these sharing of skills that make networking the powerful tool that it is.

Where can you help others? Are you willing to offer and prepared to deliver? Often, you will find partners in your networking world that will fill in where you need them because you fill in where they need you.

Set your intentions in writing. Revisit them daily. Put your intentions out there and you will attract the types of experiences and contacts you need.

Abby brings a ball everywhere she goes. She may not get to use it, but she is ready should the opportunity arise. Because of her intention, she gets to play ball more often than not.

Sniffing out the fakes

Stormy, the big black and white cat, cuddles up to Abby and licks her on the head. Abby scoots over just a little to give him enough room on her bed. She loves her kitty. They will touch noses with each other in the hallway and snuggle on the couch. Stormy is the real deal.

The new gray kitty, however, was another matter. He just wasn't interested in being friends with her. Sure, he'd tolerate being near her – but only if there was a treat involved. She knew he truly did not like her, so she did not even try to nose him in the hallway.

Abby meets and greets everyone, but she is very particular with whom she truly befriends. She can easily sniff out anyone who is just being nice to her but doesn't mean it, even if they try to give her a treat. She may not understand it, but she does not like to be sold any more than you do.

Frankly, if networking were simply selling there would be nothing but tire-kicking and pyramid building going on anywhere you went.

Networking is not only done at events set up for that purpose. While these events are great places to meet people and practice, you do not turn out the lights and close the door on your networking as soon as the event is over. You are always on. This is why you must always be YOU.

You will never see Abby pretending to be a Chihuahua. She just is who she is, and yet she attracts other dogs and owners by being herself. She doesn't go out of her way to try to fit in. Even when she is surrounded by cats, she doesn't try to meow.

If you are a plumber who normally wears coveralls, why would you wear a tuxedo to network? It doesn't fit you or your job. In fact, it may make people distrust you. Yes, you should absolutely be professionally dressed, but above all, be comfortable. You represent no one but yourself.

This is where people lose focus on what, exactly, networking is. Sure, you are there to meet people and promote your business, in a way. That is an after-effect, not your main objective while face-to-face with other human beings.

Networking is about relationships, first and foremost. You cannot build trusting relationships unless you are willing to be yourself.

Hoarding toys

When Abby was a puppy, she went through a chewing phase. One evening, while visiting my parents, my dad came downstairs and said that Abby had chewed on one of his work shoes. In her defense, I pointed out that there were two other dogs and my sister's puppy in the house – how did he know for sure it was Abby?

"Because," he said, handing me a tennis ball, "she left her calling card inside it."

Abby loves tennis balls. There are tennis balls all over the house, the yard and even our car. Her way of letting you know she likes you is to lay a tennis ball at your feet. Wherever we go, even if we are not playing fetch at the time, she manages to find a tennis ball. I don't know how she does it.

The important thing is that Abby uses every ball she finds. For Abby, being a Retriever is not just about collecting tennis balls.

For you, networking is not just about collecting business cards.

In your networking career, you will have the opportunity to collect a lot of business cards. But it is what you do with each one, not how many you have, that will ultimately build your network.

Truly, the more people you know, the better – but the operative word here is KNOW. The most important thing you will do in your networking career is refer others. You want to know that your referral will be good one. Your own reputation is on the line!

Do take the card, but also write yourself notes on it as to where you met and why you are interested in following up with this person.

Remember, even a ball-obsessed Retriever doesn't just stash her collection. She has her favorites that she returns to, but she still uses every ball she's collected at every possible opportunity.

Burying bones

Abby has a way of planting tennis balls in convenient places to ensure that you understand there WILL be fetching at some time. Instead of obvious places, such as the middle of the hallway or her toy box, you might find one on the chair in which you are about to sit, in your purse or floating in her water dish. No matter the time or place, if you say, "Where is it?" she can bring you a tennis ball.

Abby invests in her future.

Much like Abby's painstaking tennis ball planting, building a network is like investing in your future. Building a good network begins with finding quality, reliable sources for the things you need. You already have a network, and you may not even know it. Think about your dentist, the guy who painted your mom's house or your hairdresser. Need a good mechanic? Start by asking your family, friends and, yes, even your dentist. You'll find that a well-built network loops back on itself.

As you can see, these relationships can lead to business contacts, new friends, referrals for services and sometimes job connections. If you only collect a business card and move on, you have not made a connection.

How many cards have you kept in your purse, pocket or wallet that you haven't the faintest idea why? Do you remember the conversations that led up to you asking for those cards?

I am part of a marvelous little business network group called the Kent Breakfast Club[1]. Each week we gather for an early breakfast and practice our networking. Each member gives a 30-second commercial for his or her businesses or products. After that, we have a prepared speaker and some business items. The best part comes at the end, when we can give a public thank you to someone in the group who may have either referred us or helped us during the week. Gratitude is the juiciest, most effective part of networking.

We take the time to get to know each other both inside and out of our businesses. My personal life and my business have both been enriched by the members of this club.

Like any investment, it may take some time to reap returns. But, even when the returns are slow in coming, that doesn't mean you stop investing. The rewards may trickle or they may gush, but always reinvest. Refer folks from your network to others. Check up on the friends you've made. Go to functions where you may get to see these people again. Inform them of new developments in your business or life.

All investments – stocks, homes, children, pets, networks – must be nurtured.

Part 2
Untuck Your Tail
Overcoming social anxiety

Even cats can UN-learn

When we first combined households, Abby was ecstatic that she got a new friend, Jim's gray and white cat, Junior Barnes.

Junior was not so thrilled.

Junior, much like Jim, had been a bachelor his entire life and was perfectly happy on his own. All of a sudden, there was a new human, cat AND dog cluttering up his social arena and making him quite uncomfortable. He went into fits of anxiety - spitting, sputtering, hissing and hiding. He was a nervous wreck.

The girl and the cat weren't so bad, but the dog just wasn't his scene. With gentle coaxing and Abby's classic ignoring technique (read more in "Growlers vs. alphas"), Junior did come around. In fact, now he is so social that we couldn't get him OUT of the picture when doing the photo shoot for the cover of this book. Junior unlearned his shyness.

Like any relationship, networking takes time and effort. For someone who is not an extrovert, this may seem daunting, but it truly isn't. The great thing about networking is that you can take it at your own pace and your network will still grow exponentially. Much like driving or reading, once you learn the basic principles you will get better at it the more you do it.

Well-adjusted domestic dogs are master networkers. They are not shy. It is part of their nature. Dogs are pack animals, meaning they particularly enjoy being with others.

Human beings are pack animals as well. We seek out others; we desire to be around other people. No other species experiences loneliness more frequently or profoundly than human beings. We are hard-wired to share space, time and events with other humans.

Why is this so important to networking? Simply put, because no one is born shy[2]. Unless you have a genuine chemical imbalance, your shyness is a learned trait.

This is wonderful news!

If your shyness is a learned trait, it means that you can UN-learn it!

Think of any habit you have had to break or any new job you have had to learn. With patience and practice, you stopped or started and moved on. You can do this with your social anxiety.

What stands in your way? Start with your parents – they told you to never talk to strangers and wait to be properly introduced. This makes networking seem counterintuitive, doesn't it? These are the same people that taught you to never take candy from strangers - unless you dressed up like a princess or cowboy first and rang their doorbell to threaten them for it. No wonder you're confused! But, don't worry – you are not alone.

Forget what your parents taught you when you were a child. They did their best to protect you as a child in an adult world. Now, you are a grownup in that same world, and it's time you made your own rules. You can succeed at networking and open far more opportunities than you ever thought possible.

First, you must learn to fearlessly meet new people.

Breeding vs. attitude

Bounding up to the little Shih Tzu, Abby expected to make a new friend. After all, her best friend in the whole, wide world is her 'cousin,' my sister's Shih Tzu, Jezzy. Because of growing up with Jezzy, Abby loves all small dogs. She was especially upset when this particular little dog turned around and bit her nose!

Have you ever been snapped at by a Schnauzer, pounced by a Poodle or bitten by a Beagle? We have all experienced meeting the best of the breed – a papered, registered, gorgeous specimen of impeccable pedigree, and a total pain in the tail. What is it that a sweet, intelligent mutt has that a fancy, pampered show-breed doesn't?

It's all in the attitude.

Abby is indeed a purebred, but it was Abby's attitude that made me pick her from a large litter of puppies. Her attitude has helped me through some of the roughest times of my life, and her attitude is what lands her new friends every day.

Abby doesn't give up, never gives in, and always assumes the answer will be, "Yes." Abby believes in the goodness of every person or pet that she meets (yes, even cats). She minds her manners. Abby goes into every situation with positive intention.

Your résumé, testimonials, branding, experience, education, fashion sense, location, contacts or net worth mean nothing to others if YOU don't match your intention. You are the most important sales and marketing tool you have.

It is your ability to make lasting impressions and build relationships that close deals, retain customers, move you up the corporate ladder and set the stage for success.

It is your attitude that determines your success.

You are reading this book because you genuinely want to succeed. You are already halfway there. Now, take that desire and make it your intent. This is your attitude of success.

Abby does not desire to be a good dog, she intends it. She sets out with purpose to do what a good doggy does, and she is successful at it. Every time we celebrated her success – with a treat or a simple "good girl" – we drove her closer to her goal. She no longer has to look for outside approval, she knows she's on the right track – but she still gets plenty of treats and kudos anyway because she deserves them.

Here is a secret about your attitude: it can be cultivated with positive reinforcement. Yes, just like Abby, you can treat yourself into a good attitude!

Negative reinforcement does not work with Abby. When she was a puppy, I would have never been able to train her using spanking or punishing – it only made things worse.

This is true for people on so many levels. Dwelling on what should have happened but didn't happen makes it so that nothing happens. Yet, celebrating anything that goes well – no matter how small – works wonders.

Do this for yourself. Learn from your mistakes, but celebrate each and every success. If you are on the right track, cheer yourself on to more. Treat yourself, give yourself "good girls" (or boys) and you will see a new attitude with a stronger intention and a lot more success.

Chasing your tail

The first time Abby noticed her tail, she was 9 weeks old. She chased it around and around, and then realized both were going nowhere fast. She has never chased her tail again.

One of the hardest things for a novice networker to do is decide where to start. The best way to determine your starting point is to determine where not to begin. Do not begin in a place that leaves you chasing your tail. While you may meet some great folks at a grocery store, baseball game, college course or gym, these are not optimal networking environments. Not yet.

Start with places that you can meet like-minded people and where you can feel comfortable even when nervous. It's easier to talk to strangers when you know that you already have a common interest or passion. Remember how Junior Barnes loved the camera? His passion for being in pictures gave him the extra courage he needed to face The Dog.

Look for business clubs that focus on your field, join an educational club such as Toastmasters[3], or attend a smaller local event such as a book club or wine tasting. These are all great for beginners. Don't forget your church, school or worksite – you will be amazed at the nearly hidden opportunities to network.

If you want to meet amazing people and help your community, join a philanthropy group such as the Kiwanis[4], volunteer for fundraisers such as a cancer walk[5] or get involved with an organization like World Vision[6]. Pick your passion and you will find networking comes naturally.

When you feel a bit more confident, discover your local Chamber of Commerce, a more comprehensive business club, or the higher levels of the clubs you have already joined. Get involved – serve on a board or start a program.

Do not allow yourself to get wrapped up in an organization's politics or talked into something you do not want to do. Remember, you are doing this to develop your social and business contacts, not run yourself in circles.

There are millions of opportunities out there that can help build your confidence and contacts that don't leave you chasing your tail.

Touching noses

Abby was the only canine at a child's birthday party, but she was more popular than the clown. Kids and parents alike were delighted by the sweet Retriever that came and said hello.

The first thing Abby does when entering a room is walk around and say hello. She does this in a non-threating way that tends to endear even non dog-friendly folks. When she returns to a place she's worked before, familiar dogs greet her with a nose touch and many people actually say hello to her FIRST.

Why? Because she is happy to see them, and people like to be liked.

This is your goal. When you walk into a room, first look around to see if you know anyone. If you do, give them a greeting – even if it is a simple nod, smile or wave from across the room. Then, greet those that are in charge or there to help – the doorman, the registrar, the waitress, the host. Get your bearings. Finally, walk around the room and meet those you don't yet know - just a quick hello and smile, the human equivalent of a nose touch. If you meet someone wonderful, you can get back to them.

Always remember to smile.

One of Abby's best assets is her smile. While the baring of teeth can mean the opposite in the wild, it has been shown that dogs will, indeed, learn to utilize the facial expressions of their owners[7]. We then reward them by our reaction – joy and/or petting. This is how virtually every trick a dog learns is reinforced. Positive feedback works wonders.

A smile translates through nearly every culture. Smiling is an invitation that tells the other person you like them, no strings attached.

Your smile is positive feedback to strangers.

Offerings

"What is this?" the fellow at the fountain asks, looking at the wet, slimy ball between his feet. "Are you offering me a present, girl?" With closed eyes and a look of pure ecstasy, Abby leans into the man scratching behind her ears. "You know," he tells me with an amused and slightly bewildered look, "I honestly don't really like dogs. I'm not sure how I ended up in this position, but I don't mind. I really like this one."

How do you become the kind of dog that even cat-lovers want to pet?

Begin by introducing yourself.

These days, hardly anyone knows how to properly introduce another person. Remember when your parents told you to never speak until spoken to? If you listen to your parents' advice now, you may be waiting a LONG time to be introduced in a new environment.

If Abby stood back and waited to be introduced to everyone, she would never get belly rubs or ear scritches. She never waits; she goes right up and introduces herself first. She makes more friends than any man, woman or mutt on the planet.

In lieu of a slimy ball, offer your own introduction. Start with "Hello, my name is …, and _____." Fill in the blank with something inviting. The best way to invite people into conversation is to give them a way to help you. For instance, "I just moved here from Michigan."

It seems simple, but it is so effective.

You are indeed giving them a gift. People genuinely want to help one another, even if it is just making them feel welcome in a new place.

Another way to offer something is to compliment a person. For instance, the easiest conversation starter in the world is to remark on someone's jewelry. An interesting necklace or beautiful ring always has a story behind it. Without fail, you will engage your new friend in a stimulating conversation simply by offering her a way to express herself. You have given her a gift, and she will return in kind.

Remember, though, to always be yourself. Abby can't offer much more than a used ball or a tail wag, but it is authentic and it works for her. What do you have to offer?

Apologizing is for puppies

Abby recently met a young Chocolate Lab at the river, cute little guy. Abby wanted to play, but whenever she got near him, he cowered and shrank away. When Abby was chasing a stick or playing with another dog, the little Chocolate was enrapt. He really did want to play. But, whenever one of them approached him, he just lowered his eyes and backed away. It was as if he were constantly apologizing for his existence.

Abby soon lost interest in him because it seemed to her that he didn't want to play.

Apologizing lacks professionalism and makes you appear weak. It is off-putting and sometimes makes people lose interest in you. This is quite the opposite of what you are trying to convey.

Regardless of your background or culture, when it comes to networking, you must be direct and confident. Speak up! Join in! You are worth another person's time. You are not imposing. You are every bit as witty, intelligent and important as the person to whom you are speaking.

When in a group, speak with authority. Your opinion matters. People would not be in a group if they weren't looking for interaction with others.

They want to know about your job, your business or your expertise. There is always someone looking for what it is that you do. Do not be sorry for speaking.

"I'm sorry" is not the only way you convey your apologies. Keep track of the phrases that you use when you are nervous. Many may not feel like apologies to you, but they sound like it to others. Here are some examples:

- This is just my view/opinion, but …

- I'm just thinking that …

- I could be totally wrong about this, but …

- I'm not trying to pretend I'm some kind of expert, but …

Using "just" or "but" a lot may mean to you that you are trying to soften or modify your statement, yet it translates to others that you do not truly believe in what you are saying. You are pre-apologizing! Be wary of using these modifiers. Instead, be bold and unapologetic in your statements. However, do make sure that you are speaking on topics of which you truly are knowledgeable. No one likes know-it-alls, especially when they are wrong.

If you have a need, ask boldly. What is the worst that can happen? Really, what is the worst thing that could possibly happen, and how bad is that, honestly? People are often so busy figuring out how to take "No" for an answer that they are not prepared to accept a "Yes." Do not be afraid to ask, ever! The potential gains far exceed the possible risks.

Be your sweet, humble self, even if you are socially awkward – and don't apologize for it.

Later that same day, we got to see a puppy grow up a little right before our very eyes. The Chocolate simply couldn't take it anymore. He jumped into the water and grabbed one end of the stick that Abby was playing with. They got into a tug of war and then happily splashed all over in full play mode.

Because he got over his apologetic state, he was able to go boldly for what he wanted – and he got it!

Let's play -- Entering a conversation

When Abby bounds up to a group of dogs or people, she easily engages them in doggy conversation, usually involving tennis balls or stick tug-of-war. Dogs are perpetual three-year-olds mentally. It is easy for them to engage in play with even complete strangers. Would that it were so easy for us humans!

When you think about it, three is the age that we humans begin to explore our relationships and learn social skills – we are fearless at that age. Dogs never outgrow their social skills. Why do we?

When in a networking situation, there are several ways to enter an existing conversation without feeling awkward.

First, pay attention to body language. Abby does not approach dogs that are snarling or hiding between their master's legs. Neither should you approach a group that is in a 'closed' conversation. You can easily see when a conversation is closed by looking at the participants' feet and/or shoulders. Are they pointing in, towards one another? If so, then the group is most likely engaged in a closed conversation, meaning it may be personal or they just do not want to engage anyone else at this point.

If their feet and/or shoulders are pointing slightly away from one another, then the group is engaged in an open conversation, meaning they are open to others joining them. Use the physical opening and one of these methods:

The tried and true

Remember your introductory gift? Simply approach the group and say, "Hello, my name is _____."

The Greet and Meet

Greet someone familiar in the group and have them introduce you to the rest.

The Drive-by Eavesdrop

Without actually eavesdropping, casually see if you can pick up something that might give you an opening. A question is best, and it does not have to pertain to business at all. Make sure that your question is open-ended, meaning they cannot give you a one-word answer.

The Acting Host

Abby meets everyone at the door as if she were the host – and no one has ever questioned her. At large events, it is rare to meet the actual host, if there is one. Without alluding to the idea that you are, in fact, the host of the event, greet people in the group as if you were, "I am so glad you could make it this evening. Aren't they doing a great job? How do you like the salmon puffs?"

The first time you attempt joining in, it may be scary – but remember, you are learning a new skill. Just like the first time you tried to ride a bicycle, it may be a little shaky, but hang in there. With just the tiniest bit of practice, you'll be up and rolling.

Taking your ball home -- Exiting a conversation

When Abby is done playing or tired of a playmate, she simply grabs her ball and walks away or sits on the ball until the other dog gets the hint. We humans have to be a little more diplomatic.

Now that you know how to enter a conversation, it is imperative that you be able to exit one. Why stay in a conversation or situation that may hinder your ability to meet your goal for the event? No matter how witty or engaging the person you are talking to may be, you do not want to spend the entire event without meeting others.

Why would you stay in one spot with one person? Most likely, you are too polite or afraid that you might offend the other person – or you may simply not know how to escape.

There are some simple methods that you may practice to make your escape, without making enemies.

First of all, no matter which method you choose, remember to never just turn your back. You do not want the person to feel 'ditched' – even if politely so. A good rule to remember is the ¼ rule. Always move to a distance at least ¼ the size of the room away. This makes it appear that you do, in fact, have a purpose "way over there."

Another rule to follow is to never make promises you cannot or do not want to keep. These are easily recognizable brush-offs that also make the other person feel ditched. Never say you will call someone that you don't want to meet again. Do not offer favors or set 'sometime' dates for lunch. If you truly do want to meet for lunch, set a date on the spot.

With these tips in mind, choose one of the following methods for your exit:

Just Leave

There are several variations of just taking your ball and going home, including:

Excusing yourself

The most common exit statement is simply, "Excuse me," then move on (remember, ¼ of the room away).

The other person

Point out someone that you need to speak to, say good bye, and go to them.

The compliment

Politely tell the other person how interesting and engaging the conversation was, and that you do not want to monopolize them the entire evening. You are sure that so-and-so would like to meet them.

Nature calls

You are human, and you will at some point need to use the facilities or refresh your drink. These are perfectly respectable reasons to end the conversation and disappear for a bit.

The rescue

You see a friend (at least ¼ of the room away!) who needs you to help them in some way. Some examples are that your friend needs an introduction to someone else or you have something that they need.

The meet & switch

Be sure that your body language shows that you are in an open conversation. Invite in another person, introduce yourself and your new friends, and then leave when they begin talking to each other. This works best with someone you have met before so that you may give thoughtful introductions.

The bring-along

Simply invite them along to meet someone else at the other end of the room. This can work to your favor in two ways. Either the person will decide that they are happy where they are and you are free to go speak to the other person on your own, or they will choose to follow you, whereupon you can use the meet & switch with the other person.

With just a little practice, these tactics become second nature and will not offend the other person. The trick is to leave every person, every time, assuming you have his/her best interests at heart. Even when Abby takes her ball and sits on it, she leaves her playmate knowing that she had the best intentions and they will play again.

Part 3
Sit. Shake. Speak.
...and other tricks of the advanced networker

Be a good dog

Abby has many human aunts and uncles, and her favorite is Aunt Lexy. Whenever Aunt Lexy is around, Abby gets all riled up and wants to jump all over her, even though she knows better. Sometimes we have to tell her, "No!" so that she'll back off a bit. At that point, she does not persist, she backs off. Aunt Lexy will then administer the proper attentions.

Remember the networking vs. marketing difference? This is where you draw the line. It is usually subtle, but easily spotted when you are paying attention. People will have nearly the same reaction to an overzealous sales pitch as they will to a spastic dog. They want you to back off.

You do not have to be the center of attention to be noticed and remembered. Abby gets the most attention when she's being perfectly quiet and obedient. Yes, the dog that jumps about or humps the furniture gets attention – but not good attention.

People want to get away from overzealous sales people. They do not remember them in a good light. They do not want to associate with them for any longer than they must. This is not effective networking!

You want the good attention.

It is the good dogs that people remember. It is the good dogs that people go to events to see. It is the good dogs that get invited to more play dates. It is the good dogs that are the most successful.

When someone says "No," they mean it. Back off! Don't persist. Don't growl, snap or bite. Be a good dog and you will make a good impression. This opens you up to more possibilities in the future.

Growlers vs. alphas

"I locked up Toby because I didn't know how he'd react to Abby being here. He tends to be aggressive and pick fights," my mother-in-law told me during our recent visit. I reassured her that Abby would do one of two things: completely ignore him or walk away. I began to tell her that Abby does not deal well with aggression, but I corrected myself. Actually, experience has shown that she deals perfectly with aggression.

Some dogs have a natural tendency to dominate any other dog in the region, even if there is no competition. These are not necessarily alpha dogs, they are just aggressive. They face off against any dog – even bigger ones – because they are insecure about their position in the pack.

When faced with an aggressive personality, keep in mind that you are facing someone with severe insecurities. They are trying to protect something that is not in danger and is not theirs to guard. They are not alpha; they are children trying to act alpha. A true alpha does not have to use aggression to get his or her point across. A natural leader is able to communicate more effectively.

Mom did finally let Toby loose, and he beelined to Abby with hackles raised. Abby had a little girl tossing a ball for her, she couldn't care less

35

about Toby's display. Even as he followed her, sniffed her and let out a growl here and there – she completely ignored him. Once he realized that he wasn't getting a reaction out of her, he began to run after the ball, too. Soon, the two dogs had three balls and four kids between them having a blast. Mom was amazed at how well Toby handled the entire evening.

When dealing with an aggressive personality, use the same tactics that Abby uses – ignore them. Let them growl and snap and make complete fools out of themselves. Once they realize that no one is listening, they will calm down and sometimes even enjoy the event.

Positioning

Abby and I love lunch at the Kona Kai. She is content to lie next to me as I work on my laptop and we share a chicken Caesar salad. Well, the chicken, anyway. I must have been working too hard because I suddenly realized that she was no longer lying near me. One minute she was completely comfortable next to me by the window, the next minute she's on the cold tiles in front of the exit. She did this very subtly. Why?

I realized that I had just witnessed Abby make the ultimate networking move. Not a moment later, a group of friendly people got ready to exit, meaning they would have to walk right past her. Of course, there was much oohing and ahing over the sweet dog in the path, and Abby got many pets and belly rubs from several strangers.

Later that same day, a group of young men came in for a meeting. The first one eyed Abby and called her over. In less than a minute, Abby had wriggled her way into the middle of the group, bent around the table, and was getting petted by no less than four boys at a time.

Abby understands strategic positioning.

When you want to meet people, you cannot hide in a corner and expect people to find you. Get out of your comfort zone. Go out into the room, away from your friends and away from the familiar. Mingle; use some of your new conversation-entry skills. You never know who you will meet.

Don't be afraid of the big dogs

It's not often that Abby has competition for a game of fetch, but the puppy that joined us that day gave her a run for her money. Not quite a year old, the puppy outweighed Abby by at least 30 pounds. With long, gangly legs and jaws big enough to swallow her head, he could have scared her into a hole. Instead, she treated him like the puppy he was.

Abby did not care that this dog could squash her like a grape. He was fun, and she treated him like any other dog. She knows that no matter how big the dog, at the end of the day, they still drink from the same dish.

Great Dane or Mastiff, Abby will play with them all. Yes, they can be intimidating, but rarely are they mean simply because of their stature. Some dogs command more authority than others, but when it comes down to it, a dog is a dog.

When you are facing a big dog, say, the marketing lead of a company you're interested in, a movie star or the governor of your state, there is no reason to be afraid or mousy. When it comes down to it, a person is a person.

Treat them as you would any other person – with respect and friendly interest. Remember, at the end of the day, you were at the same watering hole.

39

Leashing yourself

While walking downtown one day, we happened across an angry man. We figured he was angry because he unleashed a string of swear words as we neared him. Abby did not like this rude behavior, so she took her leash in her mouth and started to lead me the other away. The man must have recognized her indignation, because he ended up apologizing first to Abby, then to me for his display.

Many laws have been made to ensure that dogs are leashed. While most people think it is to protect the people from the dogs, leashes mainly protect the dogs from all the other dangers around them.

Humans have a tendency to get themselves into trouble if they are not leashed. For some, there should be a tongue-leash law. While humans have the most developed form of communication, we also have developed the most complex means of misunderstanding each other. Wars have been waged on these miscommunications.

If you want to invest in yourself via networking, remember that you are always 'on.' You cannot run amok and say or do whatever you want. Even when a bully dog growls at you, remember to be a good dog. It may not seem like anyone is watching, but others will see and take note.

Leash yourself. You can't always say exactly what you want to say, just as Abby cannot and most likely should not run everywhere she desires.

Going bye-bye

As soon as she hears the car keys, Abby is by the door with a ball in her mouth. She doesn't care where we are going, she's just happy to go, period.

Abby is willing to go to so many more places than just the dog park, and she makes the best of each place she goes. Abby will network no matter where she is. If I throw her in the back of the car on the way to the gas station, she will meet and greet anyone she can touch noses with. This is how you should operate.

Networking everywhere you go is far more effective than only going to the events set up specifically for networking. You may have started in smaller groups or events, but now you are an advanced networker. Now you can network at the grocery store, baseball game, college course or gym. In fact, you may be networking so naturally that you don't even recognize it anymore!

Touch noses everywhere you go. Do not be afraid to be proud of who you are and what you do. You never know when that person in line behind you just needed a smile to make their day, or the person in line ahead of you really needed your product at this moment.

Whenever you go bye-bye, be prepared. Always have a few of your cards on you (even when jogging in the park) and always be genuine.

Make the most of every outing.

Paws in the air

All day long, Abby chased balls, swam and played with kids. Finally, after a long day in the sun, she had had enough. When someone tried to grab the ball from her, she sat on it so he couldn't throw it again. The rest of the evening, while people walked, talked and played all around her, she rested on her back with all four paws in the air.

Abby runs hard, plays hard and enjoys every possible second. She can play fetch for hours, but eventually she stops and sits on the ball.

Abby is able to stop and rest without an ounce of guilt. When she goes inside she drinks deeply and then she rests. She does not make excuses for her need to rest. Abby knows that great bursts of industriousness are only effective with adequate amounts of rest.

Allow yourself to rest. In fact, make yourself rest. Rest is not a time to feel guilty; it is a time to feel cherished. You should always cherish yourself. Remember the oxygen mask principle on airplanes – always put yours on first, before you try to save anyone else. You are worth more to others when you take care of yourself first.

You do no one any good if you are exhausted. You do not impress anyone in or out of your network with how long you can run on empty. If you are brain-drained and grumpy, you will not be able to remember names, connections or ideas. Plus, you do not leave a good impression – which defeats your networking purpose.

When Abby runs out of energy, she will sometimes bring back the ball at a slow walk. That's not fun. Networking with big, black bags under your eyes is no fun, either. You deserve a break!

Part 4
Happy Tails
Tips and extras

Follow up

While in a meeting with a business associate in my home, she looked down to discover that she had a tennis ball in her briefcase. Without comment, she absently tossed it aside and fished out a pen. Later, she bent to grab some paperwork and found the ball had returned. She tossed it aside again. Within a few minutes, she looked down to find TWO tennis balls in her briefcase. To her right, Abby sat looking at her expectantly. "You realize," I said with a smirk, "you are playing a very slow version of fetch."

"I must say," she replied, "I wish my sales team had such great follow-up."

Every time you take or give a card or make a promise to meet up later, you are playing a slow game of fetch. Don't leave the other party hanging. Bring back the ball and put it in their court (or briefcase). Never let an opportunity pass to follow up with a new contact.

Never spam. Do not sell. Instead, simply engage and be gracious. Learn a bit about the other person. Remember, networking is two-way.

The next time the associate visited, she brought a dog treat in her purse.

Good follow-up is always returned with opportunity.

Treats

One year Abby got to go trick-or-treating. People loved seeing a 10-year-old Darth Vader and his dog with a cat costume so much that he'd get a treat and Abby would often get a bone or table scrap. By the third house, she had it all figured out. To this day, if in a strange neighborhood, I have to maneuver her away from people's front doors or she will ring their doorbells expecting a treat.

Abby also has the coffee lady, the bank lady and the guys at the post office figured out. She knows that with good networking, she gets extra treats.

One of the benefits of being a good networker is that people will give you treats. These may come via referrals, discounts for products or services, something extra in your order and sometimes even a flat-out goodie from someone who appreciates you. You may learn of new opportunities or upcoming events. You may even get invited to coffee or lunch.

These are gifts among friends; never accept anything that smells like a bribe. These small and thoughtful treats mean that you have formed relationships that last – you have achieved your networking goals.

Remember to always follow up with a thank you!

Always retrieve

Abby ran like a gold-red steak and jumped gracefully in midair, snapping her jaws fiercely, only to completely miss the ball. Landing clumsily, she did a near-summersault, then jumped to her feet and immediately began searching for the ball so that she could return it for another try.

When Abby plays fetch, she tries, God love her, to catch the ball mid-air, but manages to grab it only once in a while. She usually gets it on the first bounce. Sometimes it bops her in the nose, rolls down the back of her head, and lands in the field behind her. The great thing about her, though, is that no matter how humiliating the catch, she always brings back the ball. Even if she misses it entirely, she still comes back with the prize.

So often, if something is not easy for us humans the first time (catching it in the air) or at least kind of easy the first or second time (catching it on the bounce) we just give up (leave it in the field)! Why on earth do we even bother to try if we are just going to abandon our hard work and planning so that someone with more tenacity can come along and scoop it up behind us? Humiliation and failure are not the end results, they are merely learning tools. Use them and do not give up on your goal.

Keep your eye on the ball, even if it bounces off of your nose and lands behind you. Just because you missed it does not mean you should leave it behind for some other dog to retrieve. In fact, if you look around hard enough, you might be able to scoop up the balls left behind by all those others that gave up and came back with nothing.

Abby brings back extra balls all the time.

Social media mixed-breed

Even Abby spends some time on the internet, and its influence certainly cannot be ignored. Many of the real-time networking contacts you make may start on the internet, but, as this book points out, that is not where it should end. Many of the same etiquette principles of in-person networking apply to on-line networking. The most important principle to carry over is leashing yourself.

Always remember, the internet is *not* Vegas. Whatever happens on the internet STAYS on the internet – forever. Whatever and whenever you post, ask yourself: "Is this something I want my mother / spouse / pastor / kid / boss to read?" If not, DON'T post it. One or all of them will find it. Even if you delete it, it will be recovered. The internet never forgets.

Internet trails are not like vapor, they are more like tattoos. Even when surgically removed, they leave visible & recognizable scars.

When approaching a social media site, begin by "lurking and learning." This means reading a lot before you even set up a profile. Take your time to get to know a site before you get involved.

Ask yourself:

- What is the personality of the site?

- Are these the types of people I want as friends or customers?

- What questions are they asking, and can I be a resource?

Once you have found a site or two (not more, as you won't have time to devote to too many), build your profiles. Be concise and complete. Don't accept the defaults, meaning, use your brand. If you don't have a brand, go back and start by creating one. Take the time to make your profiles look and feel like your own website – and make sure they all point to one another. If you don't have a website, go back and create one.

Finally, engage. Offer something useful. Reply to questions. Be thoughtful. Do not just use the site as a vehicle for free advertising or people will tune you out. Just like in-person networking, you want to build relationships.

Social media, upon first blush, sounds like a quick and easy way to blast your message, but it is ineffective if no one is there to hear it. Just like in-person relationships, social media takes time to nurture. By using the same basic principles you have found in this book, you can build an on-line network that is ever-expanding and beneficial to all involved.

The internet is great, but to get the most out of your business and social life, never stop networking Nose-to-Nose.

Take your time. Even the most social creature can end up a pooped pup!

Resources

[1] The Kent Breakfast Club meets every Wednesday morning at 7:30 am. Details may be found on their website: www.kentbreakfastclub.com

[2] See shyness research by Bernardo J. Carducci. Ph.D., 2008; Damon & Hart, 1982; 1988; Lewis Sullivan, Stranger & Weiss, 1989 (to name just a few)

[3] To find a Toastmasters club near you, go to www.toastmasters.org

[4] Find your local Kiwanis by visiting www.kiwanis.org

[5] For information on cancer walks, visit one of the following (you can find others by searching for "cancer walk"):
www.cancer.org
www.relayforlife.org
www.braincancerwalk.org
(Abby & Jezzy participated in the Seattle 2010 Brain Cancer Walk in honor of their grandma!)

[6] Visit www.worldvision.org for sponsorship and volunteer opportunities

[7] There are several studies on smiling demonstrated by dogs. See: Friederike Range, PhD., 2008; and don't forget Charles Darwin, 1872.

Special thanks to:

Jr. Barnes (page 13), Jezzy (page 15) and Ceasar (page 39) who appear with their parents' permissions.

Alexis Easterbrook-Lewis (Aunt Lexy), my business partner, hero and dearest friend.

Jim Moniz, my soul mate and biggest fan who renewed my creativity and kept me honest about finishing this project. I love you, Jimmy!

Maryum and Mychal Boiser, owners of the Kona Kai, where Abby and I wrote most of this book.

The members of the Kent Breakfast Club who all are great examples of true networking.

About the author

Award-winning speaker **Mélanie Hope** has over a decade of experience in the corporate world where she has developed many written works and training programs. As a survivor of domestic violence, she often volunteers her time and talents with advocacy programs and other charities.

In her free time, she loves to camp, hike, swim, ride roller coasters and read. An accomplished musician, she sings whenever possible and is fulfilling a lifetime ambition by learning to play the drums. She shares her life with her true love, Jim, two very personable cats and, of course, Abby.

Mélanie offers a full-day seminar further exploring and practicing the principals in Nose-to-Nose Networking. She is also available for keynote speeches. If you wish to book Mélanie for an event, contact her via **HopeSpeaking.com**

Abigail Hope is a three-year-old Golden Retriever who loves children, swimming and chasing tennis balls. She is always happy to attend events revolving around "her" book and welcomes comments on her Facebook page: www.facebook.com/nose2nose

YOU'VE READ THE BOOK
NOW EXPLORE THE CONCEPTS IN DEPTH

Engaging and fun keynote presentations include:

- Ditch the dog and pony shows - networking with intention
- Meet and greet without anxiety
- Tooting your own horn without hitting sour notes
- Social Media for the very, very beginner

Combine them all for a powerful workshop.

Nose-to-Nose the book is only the beginning!

BOOK MÉLANIE TO SPEAK FOR YOUR NEXT EVENT.

GO TO

www.HopeSpeaking.com
FOR DETAILS

8380798R0

Made in the USA
Charleston, SC
04 June 2011